Great Smoky
National

POCKET GUIDE

Randi Minetor

Photographs by Nic Minetor

FALCON GUIDES ®

GUILFORD, CONNECTICUT
HELENA, MONTANA
AN IMPRINT OF THE GLOBE PEQUOT PRESS

FACT SHEET

Established: 1934.

Visitation: In 2005, 9,192,147 people visited Great Smoky Mountains National Park, making this the most heavily visited of all 58 national parks. For comparison, Grand Canyon National Park is the second most visited, with 4.4 million annually.

Roads: 384 miles of roads crisscross the park. About 238 miles are paved, while the remaining 146 are dirt roads.

Rivers and streams: 2,115 miles of creeks, streams, and rivers flow through the park.

Waterfalls: While there are more than forty popular waterfalls in the park, many more are in the park's rivers and streams.

Visitor centers: Three are in the park at Cades Cove and Sugarlands on the Tennessee side, and at Oconaluftee in North Carolina, with another four National Park Service visitor centers in the towns of Gatlinburg (two visitor centers), Sevierville, and Townsend, Tennessee.

Buildings: Of the 342 structures within the park, 78 are historic, including the remains of early settlers' cabins, gristmills, schools, and churches from towns that stood here long before the area became a park.

Species count: About 12,000 species have been catalogued, but scientists believe there may be as many as 100,000 individual species living here, from tiny animal and plant organisms to "megafauna" like elk and bears.

Contents

Welcome:
Introduction to Great Smoky Mountains National Park

From the top of Clingmans Dome, the third highest mountain peak in the eastern United States, they stretch to the horizon in every direction—rows and rows of thickly forested ridgelines so covered with hardwoods, spruce, and fir that the foliage looks seamlessly impenetrable . . . and then, as each ridge falls away from the one before it, its deep greens fade into blues and grays that blend the bursting foliage into the range's characteristic haze. These are the Great Smoky Mountains, named "Smoky" originally for the natural pastel veil of humidity produced by so much vegetation thriving in one place, and their blue-green shroud presents more of a sense of peace than of mystery—a reminder to

◀ *On the North Carolina side of the park, the mountains are especially lush and green.*

Storm clouds fill the sky over Cades Cove.

rejuvenate, to leave our desks and cubicles and even our cars behind and surround ourselves with the bounty that this Tennessee–North Carolina border park is so ready to provide.

More than nine million people visit Great Smoky Mountains National Park every year, to drive the winding Newfound Gap Road that crosses the central ridgeline or to walk hundreds of miles of trails that lead far away from the bluster of cities and highways. Exploring the Smokies can mean a long hike into a woods where the only sounds are the "teakettle, teakettle, teakettle" call of the Carolina wren and the burble of rushing river water, tumbling over rocks and swirling between boulders on its way to the valleys below. Your exploration may take you out into the middle of one of these rivers with a fishing rod and reel, angling to catch the trout that are so plentiful in these waters. You may hike in search of one of the park's forty most popular waterfalls, or you may take to the backcountry to find the cascades that only a handful of people ever see——and whether you're in the outlands or the front country, you may finish your day in a campsite where you can see thousands of stars wink in the inky night sky.

This is hikers' nirvana, with inclines that challenge even the most experienced trekkers—but without the intimidating jaggedness of the western mountains or their equilibrium-stealing altitude. Uphill slopes lead to vistas that make you long to conquer the next ridgeline, while gentle descents into valleys bring you close to the park's famous wildlife: white-tailed does leading spotted fawns through wooded glens, splendid male elk foraging for young shoots in open fields, and the park's most sought-after large animals, the black bears, ambling through forests while their cubs scurry along fallen logs and up into the trees.

Nestled between the mountain peaks and the cove woodlands are the carefully preserved remains of villages that flourished here before and during the boom days, when logging felled millions of trees and industry clear-cut the landscape. Most of the people who lived in what is now Great Smoky Mountains National Park respected the land and used it only as a personal resource, harnessing water power to grind corn and harvesting a few trees to build homes while they grew crops to sustain their families. Their homesteads remain in Cades Cove, Oconaluftee, and Cataloochee Valley, testaments to a time when man and nature weren't at odds.

When logging threatened to eradicate these majestic forests, a group of residents led by writer Horace Kephart banded together in the 1920s to rescue this state borderland. It took the efforts of many organizations and individuals to restore the area to its original state—and today, thanks to their work, Great Smoky Mountains National Park is now the most visited of all the national parks. The union of natural beauty with hundreds of recreational choices, the abundant wildlife, the changing landscape that bursts with new color and life from one season to the next, and the astounding opportunity to enjoy this natural treasure at no charge—all of these make the Smokies the nation's number one destination for nature-loving vacationers, sparking their sense of adventure and taking them deep into one of the loveliest wilderness areas in America.

ney Whank Falls is a welcome stop on Deep Creek Trail.

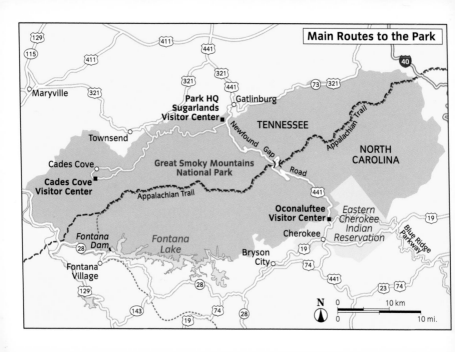

Main Routes to the Park

Maryville

Park HQ
Sugarlands
Visitor Center

Gatlinburg

TENNESSEE

Appalachian Trail

NORTH
CAROLINA

Townsend

Cades Cove

Cades Cove
Visitor Center

Great Smoky Mountains
National Park

Newfound Gap Road

Appalachian Trail

Oconaluftee
Visitor Center

Eastern
Cherokee
Indian
Reservation

Cherokee

Blue Ridge Parkway

Fontana
Dam

Fontana Lake

Bryson
City

Fontana
Village

N

0   10 km

0   10 mi.

Navigate:
Getting to and around the park

With many major cities nearby and plenty of resort areas surrounding the park, the Great Smoky Mountains are easy to reach. Rent a car if you arrive by plane or train, as you will need your own transportation to drive through this large scenic area. There are plenty of signs to direct you to the park.

Getting There and Getting Around

By air. The McGhee-Tyson Airport in Alcoa, just south of Knoxville and about 45 miles west of Gatlinburg, is the closest airport to the Great Smoky Mountains. Make a reservation with Rocky Top Tours (865-429-8687 or 877-315-8687) to take their shuttle bus to Gatlinburg.

In North Carolina, the nearest airport is the Asheville Regional Airport, about 60 miles east of the park entrance in Cherokee.

If you own or have access to a private plane, you can fly into the Gatlinburg–Pigeon Forge Aviation Center in Sevierville, just 12 miles from the park.

By bus. There is no public bus transportation from out of the area to the park. Once you arrive in Gatlinburg, the Gatlinburg Trolley can take you from town to the Sugarlands Visitor Center and/or to Laurel Falls, one of the park's paved paths, for a 1-mile walk to the falls. (Look for the trolleys on the Gold line.) You'll need your own transportation to see the rest of the park.

By train. The nearest Amtrak station is in Greenville, South Carolina, more than 100 miles from the park.

By car. From the north, take Interstate 40 south from Knoxville and drive 25 miles. Take exit 407 in Dandridge and drive on U.S. Highway 66 to Sevierville, where it becomes U.S. Highway 441. Drive on US 441 through Sevierville and Pigeon Forge to Gatlinburg. The park entrance is about 2 miles from the first Gatlinburg Welcome Center on US 441.

From Georgia and points south, take US 441 north to Cherokee, North Carolina. US 441 continues into the park as Newfound Gap Road, taking you to the Oconaluftee Visitor Center.

From the west, take U.S. Highway 129 south to Maryville, Tennessee, then turn north on U.S. Highway 321 and continue to Townsend, where you'll find the park's west entrance and the road to the Cades Cove Visitor Center.

From the east and Asheville, North Carolina, take I-40 west for 40 miles to Clyde, where you'll pick up U.S. Highway 19 going west. Take US 19 to US 441

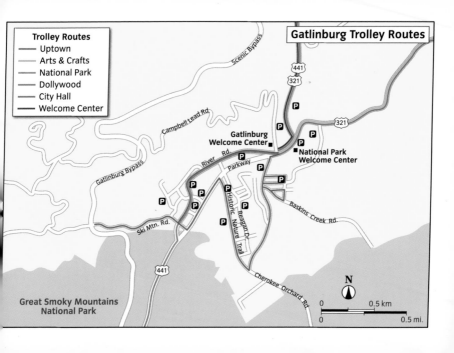

The Gatlinburg Trolley takes visitors to any point in town.

and the park's southern entrance in Cherokee.

A scenic alternative: The Blue Ridge Parkway (often called simply "the Parkway") winds for 469 miles from Shenandoah National Park in Virginia all the way to the southern (Cherokee) entrance of Great Smoky Mountains National Park. While the drive is slower (the speed limit on the Parkway is 45 mph), you'll want to proceed at a very leisurely pace so you won't miss any of the overlooks, where the foliage-covered peaks and the softly sloping valleys make this one of the nation's prettiest drives.

Park Fees and Entrances

General admission. Admission is free! Thanks to a 1936 agreement between the state of Tennessee and the federal government, there is no fee to enter the park. In that year, Tennessee completed construction of Newfound Gap Road, the park's main thoroughfare and one of the most direct and well-traveled routes through the Appalachian Mountains. To keep Newfound Gap Road accessible to Tennesseans as well as to visitors, the state demanded that the federal government maintain free passage for the life of the road.

Activity fees. Camping is $14 to $23 per night, depending on the campsite.

Park entrances. Three main entrances provide access to the park. The Gatlinburg entrance on US 441 south, on the north side of the park, leads directly to Newfound Gap Road, which crosses the park north to south. Park headquarters and the extensive Sugarlands Visitor Center are here, about 2 miles south of

You'll have no trouble finding the well-marked park entrances.

the park entrance. In Townsend, Rich Mountain Road (off US 321) leads south into the park, providing the closest entrance to the Cades Cove loop road.

The park's southern entrance is in Cherokee, North Carolina, on US 441 north, where Newfound Gap Road and the Parkway converge. The Oconaluftee Visitor Center and Mountain Farm Museum are here.

Visitor Centers

With three in-park visitor centers and four more scattered along the park's perimeter, you'll find plenty of opportunities to gather information, learn about the area's natural and cultural history, and pick up trail maps, books, souvenirs, and brochures. Six of the seven visitor centers are open every day of the year except for Christmas, while the Townsend Visitor Center closes on Thanksgiving as well as Christmas.

Sugarlands Visitor Center is the park's largest, with museum displays of meticulously preserved animals, birds, insects, and wildflowers you're likely to see in the park grouped according to habitat. Watch the short video in the center's theater to learn about the natural forces that created this park, and about the people who inhabited it over the las thousand years. Purchase water and soda here, and the bookstore (the park's largest) features the mountain area's preserves, honey, and apple butter, as well as maps and guidebooks. Restrooms and backcountry permits are available here. Open December–February from 8:30 a.m. to 4:30 p.m.; March and November from 8:00 a.m. to 5:00 p.m.; April, May, September, and October from 8:00 a.m. to 6:00 p.m.; and June–August from 8:00 a.m. to 7:00 p.m.

Cades Cove Visitor Center is about halfway around the one-way Cades Cove loop road. Here you can explore the remains of the late-nineteenth-century town and learn about authentic Appalachian life by strolling through Southern Mountain homes, a remarkable cantilevered barn, a blacksmith shop, and a working gristmill. Restrooms and a book-store are available. Open April–August from 9:00 a.m. to 7:00 p.m.; September–October from 9:00 a.m. to 6:00 p.m.; March and November from 9:00 a.m. to 5:30 p.m.; December–January from 9:00 a.m. to 4:30 p.m.; and February from 9:00 a.m. to 5:00 p.m.

What's unusual about the Oconaluftee Visitor Center is the Mountain Farm Museum located just outside, where a cluster of historic buildings from all over the Smoky Mountains have been relocated to re-create the atmosphere of a small Southern Mountain homestead. In the summer months, costumed interpreters demonstrate the daily chores of mountain farm life. A bookstore, public restrooms, water and soda machines, and backcountry permits are available here. A new visitor center building is planned here, with a projected 2010

Cantilevered barns from the 1800s are carefully preserved in Great Smoky Mountains National Park.

pening date. Open December–February from 8:30 a.m. to 4:30 p.m.; March and November from 8:00 a.m. to 5:00 p.m.; April, May, September, and October from 8:30 a.m. to 5:00 p.m.; and June–August from 8:00 a.m. to 6:00 p.m.

Outside the park, Gatlinburg has two welcome centers: one on the spur between the towns of Pigeon Forge and Gatlinburg, 2 miles north of Gatlinburg on US 441; and the Downtown Welcome Center on the parkway at traffic light number 3. Both have information about the park and all the attractions, shopping, lodging, and dining available in town. A bookstore and restrooms are available. The Downtown Welcome Center is open daily year-round from 10:00 a.m. to 6:00 p.m. The Gatlinburg Welcome Center on the US 441 spur is open November–March from 8:00 a.m. to 5:30 p.m. Hours extend April–October from 8:00 a.m. to 7:00 p.m. Sunday–Thursday and from 8:00 a.m. to 9:00 p.m. Friday–Saturday.

Looking for information on those towns on US 441 before Gatlinburg? The Sevierville Visitor Center, north of Pigeon Forge on US 441, provides brochures, maps, and guidebooks, as well as a bookstore, gift shop, and restrooms. Open Monday–Saturday from 8:30 a.m. to 5:30 p.m. and Sunday from 9:00 a.m. to 6:00 p.m.

Finally, the Townsend Visitor Center, on US 321 in Townsend, fills you in on "the peaceful side of the Smokies," in the words of Townsend's chamber of commerce, with its prime trout fishing, inner-tube rentals, and access to the Foothills Parkway—where there are some of the most spectacular views of the Smokies that can be seen from a car. Open December–February from 9:00 a.m. to

A working farm, the Mountain Farm Museum is tended by volunteers and park staff members.

4:30 p.m., March from 10:00 a.m. to 4:00 p.m., April–May and November from 9:00 a.m. to 5:00 p.m., June–October from 9:00 a.m. to 6:00 p.m. In the winter, the visitor center opens at noon on Sunday.

Visitor Services

Banks/ATMs. There are no ATM machines inside the park. Along the Parkway in Gatlinburg, ATMs are available on every block—look for the signs on shops and other buildings.

Bicycle rentals. Cades Cove campground's store rents one-speed bicycles for people who plan to cycle through the cove or in other places in the park. Call park information at (865) 436-1200 for more details.

Box lunches. Several delicatessens offer sandwiches, but the best deal in town is at Applewood Farmhouse Restaurant, at traffic light number 10 in Gatlinburg, just outside the park entrance. Applewood offers a choice of five sack lunches for $6.95, including country ham on biscuits, chicken fried to order, and a selection of fruits and cheeses. Call in your order at (865) 436-4669.

Film and camera supplies. Gatlinburg Camera, 1100 Parkway, Suite C, Gatlinburg; (865) 436-8500.

Gas stations. There's no gas available within the park boundaries, but in Gatlinburg and Townsend, you'll find Texaco stations within a quarter mile of the park entrance. The Townsend Texaco station has spotless restrooms.

Gift shops. All seven visitor centers have bookstores and gift shops run by the Great Smoky Mountains Association.

Laundry. The park has no laundry facilities. In Gatlinburg, there are two coin laundries: The Wash Tub, 642 East Parkway, (865) 436-0244, and Super Suds Coin Laundry, 1357 East Parkway. From downtown, follow Tennessee Highway 321 where it branches off the Parkway at traffic light number 3. The Wash Tub is about a mile down from this intersection, and Super Suds is another 1.5 miles after that.

Lost and found. Park headquarters, (865) 436-1230.

Medical. The Gatlinburg Family and Urgent Care Clinic, 611 Oak Street; (865) 430-7369.

Outfitters, hiking/fishing. The closest outfitter to the park is the Happy Hiker (865-436-5632), on the Parkway at traffic light number 10, just 21 feet from the park entrance in Gatlinburg. This is a popular stop for Appalachian Trail thru-hikers in May. For fishing try Smoky Mountain Angler, 466 Brookside Village Way, Suite 8, Gatlinburg, (865) 436-8746; or Smoky

The Happy Hiker, Gatlinburg

Mountain Fly Fishing Outfitters, 626 Tsali Boulevard (US 441 North), between Cherokee and Bryson City, North Carolina.

Pharmacy. Parkway Pharmacy, 917 Parkway in Gatlinburg, near traffic light number 8, (865) 436-4240.

Post office. 1216 East Parkway, Gatlinburg; (865) 436-5464.

Religious services. (All listings are in Gatlinburg.) Church of Christ, Drive at Trinity Lane, (865) 436-6504; First Baptist Church, 111 Oglewood Lane, (865) 436-4685; First United Methodist Church, 742 Parkway, (865) 436-4691; Gatlinburg Presbyterian Church, 237 Reagan Drive, (865) 436-5592; St. Mary's Catholic Church, Historic Nature Trail at Airport Road, (865) 436-4907; Trinity Episcopal Church, Historic Nature Trail at Airport Road, (865) 436-4721.

Showers. There are no showers in the park. Most commercial campgrounds in the area have showers, but they do not permit nonguests to use their facilities.

Stores and supplies. The camp store at Cades Cove campground in the park is open daily year-round from 9:00 a.m. to 7:00 p.m. Here you can buy firewood, picnic supplies, cold water and soft drinks, bread, snacks, milk, paper goods, packaged cold cuts and hot dogs, and other sundries. The grill here offers burgers, sausages, corn dogs, and chili, as well as some great soft-serve ice cream. In Gatlinburg, the Parkway Market and Deli, 1127 Parkway, (865) 436-6364, offers a more extensive selection of foods and canned goods. Whole Earth Grocery, on US 321 at 446 East Parkway #4, (865) 436-6967, carries organic foods and seasonal produce.

Park Rules, Regulations, and Safety Tips

Alcohol. Alcohol is permitted in campgrounds and picnic areas only. People in possession of alcohol must be at least twenty-one years old.

Bears. It is illegal to approach within 50 yards (150 feet) of a bear intentionally, or to disturb a bear in any way. If you're close enough to change the bear's behavior, you're too close. View bears from a safe distance with binoculars or a spotting scope. (These rules apply to all animals in the park.)

Bicycles. All roads used by automobiles are open to bicycles, but the park advises caution on all but the slowest roads. Skateboards, in-line skates, and scooters are prohibited.

Camping, backcountry. Permits, required for backcountry camping, are free and easy to obtain at any of the following locations: Oconaluftee and Sugarlands Visitor Centers; Twentymile, Big Creek, Greenbrier, and Abrams Creek Ranger Stations; Deep Creek, Smokemont, Cosby, Elkmont, and Cades Cove campground offices; Fontana Marina; Fontana Dam Visitor Center; Tremont Environmental Center; and in Cataloochee Valley near the campground.

Camping, frontcountry. In season, stays are limited to seven days, or fourteen days November 1 to May 14. Six people are permitted per campsite. No more than two motor vehicles per campsite are permitted (or one trailer and one vehicle). Quiet hours are in effect from 10:00 p.m. to 6:00 a.m., and generator use is permitted only from 8:00 a.m. to 8:00 p.m. Store all food and food-preparation equipment in your car, preferably in the trunk, or in your camper if it has solid walls (violators are subject to fines).

Firearms. All firearms and other weapons are prohibited.

Fires. Build campfires only in fire grates you'll find in campgrounds. Wood collection for fires is permitted, but only if the wood is dead and on the ground. Firewood from the following states is prohibited from entering the park by the U.S. Department of Agriculture, because dead wood from these states may harbor disease-carrying insects: Illinois, Indiana, Michigan, New Jersey, New York, and Ohio.

Fishing. You must have a license to fish in the park. (See the Resources chapter for information on where to purchase these online.)

Insects. In the fall, yellow jackets become aggressive and may sting. If you're allergic, carry an EpiPen with you. If you're stung on the hand, take off your rings immediately as swelling will occur.

Motorcycles. By Tennessee and North Carolina state laws, you must wear a helmet and ride with your headlight on.

Pets. Dogs must be kept on a leash of no more than 6 feet in length. Dogs are allowed in campgrounds and picnic areas and along roadsides, but they're permitted on only two hiking paths in the park: the Gatlinburg Trail and the Oconaluftee River Trail.

Speed limits. The park speed limit is 35 mph, unless posted otherwise.

Winding roads often require traffic to slow to 20–25 mph.

Trash. Deposit all trash in the bearproof receptacles provided. When camping or hiking in the backcountry, carry out all trash.

These trash receptacles keep the bears out.

Water. All rivers and streams in the park may contain the protozoan *Giardia lamblia,* which will show up as an intestinal disorder several weeks after you've left the park. To drink this water safely, use a filter that can remove particles as small as one micron.

Waterfall safety. Do not climb on the rocks around and above waterfalls. Rocks around the falls are covered with algae and slippery with spray, and the park records fatalities every year from falls on these rocks. Obey the posted signs.

Weather in the Park

The year-round temperate climate provides excellent recreational and scenic opportunities at any time. Temperatures can vary as much as 20 degrees from the lower elevations to the mountaintops,

Fall is a beautiful time of year to visit Great Smoky Mountains National Park.

and while the day may begin with sun, it can change to rain or snow without warning. Summers are hot and humid with highs in the 90s in the valley, cooling to pleasant 70s or 80s at higher elevations. Fall brings days in the 70s and 80s, dropping only slightly into the 50s and 60s through October and November. Winter days tend toward 50-degree weather in the valley with lows below freezing, and higher elevations see 20s and sudden snows from December through February. (See the Resources chapter for the Web site of the park's weather Webcam.)

Important Park Contact Numbers

General visitor information: (865) 436-1200

Weather forecast: (865) 436-1200, ext. 630

Emergency: 911

Backcountry camping reservations: (865) 436-1231

Backcountry information: (865) 436-1297

Frontcountry camping reservation office: (877) 444-6777

LeConte Lodge reservations: (865) 429-5704

Great Smoky Mountains Association: (888) 898-9102

History:
Key things about the park

When Continents Collide

Imagine a time more than 300 million years ago, when the current foliage-covered hillsides and verdant forests in the Great Smoky Mountains were flat, level fields grounded in sedimentary rock, deposited here by a vast, shallow ocean. It took the collision of the continents now known as North America and Africa to create the Appalachian Mountain ridgeline that stretches more than 2,000 miles from Georgia to Maine—a mountain range forced up a fraction of an inch at a time over millions of years by the tremendous pressure of one land mass pushing against another.

Such tectonic power created a craggy belt of metamorphic rock thousands of feet high—but the Appalachians are some of the world's

These sculpted mountain folds formed through millennia of erosion.

oldest mountains, and even more millions of years of rain, snow, and wind wore away the serrated peaks, leaving behind the gentler curves we see today. The mountains stood for many millennia until about 25,000 years ago, when a great glacial ice sheet crept southward from the Arctic and covered much of the northern half of what is now the United States, driving animals southward as it stole their habitat and cooled the more southerly climate. The ice sheet eventually receded and melted, but many of these mammals, reptiles, amphibians, and insects stayed in their new homes among the Smoky Mountains, turning the Smokies into one of the earth's richest regions for species diversity.

When the very first human inhabitants of North America—a nomadic people collectively known as the Paleo-Indians—arrived 12,000 years ago, they eventually settled in these hills, grew crops, and lived off the land for centuries, building permanent towns and developing the complex political structure that eventually became the foundation of the Cherokee Indian nation. Historians track the emergence of the Cherokees back to about A.D. 1000.

A Clash of Neighbors and Cultures

By the early 1500s, the Cherokee nation expanded to more than 100,000 people who lived in the eight southern states, including North Carolina and Tennessee. They lived in relative peace until the first Europeans arrived in the Appalachian Mountains—and then life began to change dramatically. Led by Hernando de Soto, a Spanish explorer on a mission to find gold in the New World, the soldiers' reputation as looters and enslavers long preceded their arrival in North Carolina's Cherokee country. Wisely, the Cherokees headed for safer ground as De Soto approached. The Spanish regiment lingered briefly and moved on, and more than two centuries would pass before significant contact between Native Americans and European descendants would take place in these mountains again.

Attracted by the promise of open land and self-sufficiency, European settlers arrived in the late 1700s, building rural communities and relying on their own ability to hunt for food, grow crops, and build homes and barns from the abundant timber. The Cherokee who inhabited these lands embraced Euro-

pean tools and customs and lived much as the white people did, but peaceful coexistence proved virtually impossible as mistrust ran rampant and violent conflicts erupted. Worse, European diseases such as smallpox decimated the tribes, fueling the Indians' anger.

The rising hostilities met a sudden end in 1830, however, when President Andrew Jackson ordered the removal of all Indian people from the southern states, decreeing that they should relocate to reservations in Oklahoma. Cherokees joined the Choctaw, Chickasaw, Seminole, and Creek tribes as they abandoned their homes—many of them forced out at gunpoint by the 7,000 U.S. military troops—and moved into temporary stockades set up by the federal government. The long walk west that followed over the winter of 1838–39, know oday as the Trail of Tears, resulted in the eaths of thousands of Indians due to isease, starvation, and exposure.

'im-ber! Logging Arrives n the Smokies

ith nearly all of the Cherokees gone— xcept for a small community recognized s U.S. citizens by the government of orth Carolina, forming the Qualla Res- rvation that shares the park's south- rn border today—the white settlers xpanded their holdings in the Southern 1ountain region, clearing wide areas of rest to make room for more crops and astureland for domestic animals. The eal impact of development and indus- y didn't come until the early 1900s, owever, when lumber corporations noved in and trees began to fall by the

thousands. With logging came people looking for work, and with the people came boomtowns that supplied the vast quantities of food, clothing, and shelter these lumber employees required.

It took fewer than twenty years for the Great Smoky Mountains region to change entirely from a quiet agrarian community to an industrial center. Railroad tracks snaked through mountain passes, provid- ing fast and easy transportation for cars laden with logs, while steam-powered equipment made the removal of cut lum- ber more efficient. As farmers abandoned their land to work in the sawmills and the dwindling forests, industry threatened to run roughshod over the entire southern Appalachian region.

Just as suddenly as it began, how- ever, the lumber boom subsided by 1930, when most of the Appalachian forests had been clear-cut and logging companies turned to the west to find fresh, unclaimed woodlands. The lumber bust forced many people to seek new employment in factories and industrial centers outside the area, while some returned to their farms, hoping to regain the self-sufficient lifestyle they enjoyed decades earlier.

What Does it Take to Make a Park?

Throughout the lumber years, as residents saw mountainsides lose their verdant foliage and stubbly pastures replace dense forests, coalitions began to form to save the land before the majesty of the Great Smoky Mountains fell before the corporate ax. In 1916 the National Park Service expressed serious interest in creating parks close to population centers so that the parks would receive local community support.

A massive fund-raising effort began to purchase the Appalachian Mountain land on the Tennessee–North Carolina border. Both state governments and scores of private citizens contributed to the cause and raised $5 million, and John D. Rockefeller closed the gap in the required funds with a $5 million donation—recognized today by a monument to Rockefeller's generosity at Newfound Gap. Later, President Franklin D. Roosevelt convinced Congress to add $1.5 million to the pot, making the final purchases of land possible and bringing the coalitions' fund-raising efforts to a close.

Finally, on June 15, 1934, Great Smoky Mountains National Park was established. The states of North Carolina

Logging denuded the landscape here, but diligent replanting brought the forests back.

and Tennessee used the funds raised to buy back the land from lumber companies, allowing the loggers to phase out operations over a period of years. The remains of some boomtowns within park boundaries became historic sites, while private landowners received special permission to continue their residency inside the park throughout their lifetimes. By the mid-1930s, peace had been restored at Great Smoky.

The job of creating a national park did not end with the dedication, however. Throughout the 1930s, more than 4,000 members of the federal government's Civilian Conservation Corps lived at the park, collected seeds from the still-forested areas, and planted millions of trees on the clear-cut hillsides. They built the park headquarters building at Sugarlands and the Oconaluftee Visitor Center, and removed hundreds of miles of railroad tracks, helping to restore the park to its current pristine condition.

Flora and Fauna:
All things great and small

With a range of altitudes, up to 85 inches of rainfall every year, more than 2,100 miles of streams and rivers, five different kinds of forests, and alpine conditions at the park's highest altitudes, Great Smoky serves as a nucleus of growth and gestation for an astonishing 12,000-plus plant and animal species—and scientists believe another 90,000 species still wait to be discovered and catalogued. So impressive is the park's list of resident species that the United Nations declared the park an International Biosphere Reserve, acknowledging its importance to the worldwide balance of man and nature.

Even if you stick to the park's main roads and most visited areas, you'll see wildlife: American kestrels and turkey vultures swooping over Cataloochee Valley, black bears and white-tailed deer foraging in the fields at Cades Cove, lungless salamanders scurrying across trails, bullfrogs jumping along the edges of streams. If you travel to the Great Smoky Mountains in April and May, wildflowers fill the meadows and cover the forest floors with blooms in every color—and in October and early November, the park displays its most spectacular colors as the leaves of more than one hundred tree species turn crimson, sienna, and gold.

The Smokies' Famous Bears

Black bears are the park's iconic resident, with more than 1,600 living here—that's two bears per square mile! The most likely places to see them are in Cades Cove and Cataloochee Valley, but you may see a bear just about anywhere in the park (watch for "bear jams"—cars stopped along the side of the road when someone has spotted a bear). While these bears appear almost diminutive when compared to the brown grizzlies in America's western parks and Alaska, the Smokies' bears generally weigh 120–250 pounds, and they are dangerous when they feel threatened. Keep your distance and don't feed them, both

Black bears are favorites with park visitors.

for your own and the bears' safety. When bears become accustomed to people food, they lose their natural wariness of humans and begin to approach cars and campsites, and this behavior can lead to auto accidents, confrontations, and injuries. (If the threat of personal injury isn't enough to deter you, this might do it: If you're caught feeding a bear, you could be fined $5,000.)

Is That a Big Deer, or an Elk?

Most of us associate elk with the western parks rather than with the Great Smoky Mountains, but the elk here—most likely in the Cataloochee Valley—were imported from the Land Between the Lakes in western Tennessee and Kentucky, and from Elk Island National Park in Alberta, Canada. Elk were reintroduced

A male elk

in this park in 2001 in an effort to repopulate a species that disappeared from these mountains more than 150 years ago. About seventy-five elk live here now, a testament to the success of this program to date. How do you tell an elk from a white-tailed deer, a much more common species in this park? The elk are much larger, heavier animals, weighing in at 700 pounds or more—compared to deer at about 100 pounds. (Also, many of the elk wear radio collars.) To see elk, drive to Cataloochee Valley around sunset, when they come out of the woods to feed in the meadows and mown grasses around the historic buildings.

Chipmunks run at top speed in park woodlands.

Lots of Furry Creatures

Raccoons, red squirrels, gray squirrels, nocturnal red and gray foxes, chipmunks, skunks, woodchucks, and even the tiny pygmy shrew make their homes here, providing hikers plenty of opportunities to encounter wildlife and observe animal behavior.

Along the rivers and streams, you may discover a river otter gliding through the water or frolicking on the bank—a rare enough find in the eastern

United States, but especially exciting here because otters were reintroduced in the 1990s. Check along the Little Pigeon River, Abrams Creek, or Cosby Creek to see these sleek swimmers.

While scientists attempted to reintroduce the red wolf to the park in recent years, the food habitat was determined to be unsuitable and the offspring were unable to survive in the wild—so the tall, doglike animal you might see along the roadside at dusk is the elusive coyote. If you're camped in the park at night, listen for the coyote's eerie howl.

Birds

If you're looking for an Acadian flycatcher, yellow-billed cuckoo, Carolina chickadee, or northern bobwhite to add to your life list, Great Smoky delivers with its diverse habitats. An avid birder can explore an alpine-level spruce forest, a mix of northern and southern hardwoods, and open, grassy fields all on the same day, racking up a species list that could number more than one hundred birds in late April and May. The temperate climate even brings fine

Ravens look distinctively different from crows—they have shorter tails and larger, heavier beaks.

winter birding, with a combination of northern and southern birds whose habitats cross at this transitional line between their breeding grounds.

Along the Smokies' peaks and ridges, birds associated with northern climates and the Canadian mountains nest and breed in the southernmost part of their range. Look for golden-crowned kinglet, red-breasted nuthatch, and northern saw-whet owl, along with winter wren, veery, and Blackburnian and Canada warblers. Ravens are common in the park, especially at high elevations: Listen for the croaking call that easily differentiates them from crows.

Lower altitudes bring a thrilling mix of southern species, such as yellow-throated vireo, scarlet and summer tanager, Acadian flycatcher, indigo bunting, ovenbird, and Louisiana waterthrush. Open fields make up only a tiny percent-

age of the park's abundant habitat, but the concentration of meadowlands in Cades Cove and Cataloochee Valley brings some very productive birding. Even the most casual observer will see hawks soaring overhead and wild turkey pecking their way across an expansive field. Eastern bluebird, eastern meadowlark, killdeer, field sparrow, and northern bobwhite can be seen here at almost any time of year. See the Resources chapter for an online checklist of birds.

Salamander Capital of the World

What other park can claim thirty different salamander species? Of the many varieties you may encounter on a walk in the woods, twenty-four are "lungless" salamanders, creatures that truly have no lungs and breathe through blood essels in their skin and in the walls of heir mouths and throats. Turn over a rock on a trail and you may find one of these bizarrely amazing creatures underneath it, or keep a close eye on the edges of streams and trails for tiny movements that may betray a salamander's presence.

Synchronous Fireflies, and When to See Them

Not many places on earth can offer a dependable display of fireflies that flash in perfect unison, but the annual appearance of synchronous firefly beetles in the Great Smoky Mountains is so popular that the park schedules trolley transportation to help control the crowds. For two weeks of evenings in mid-June, the Gatlinburg Trolley takes visitors from Sugarlands Visitor Center to the Little River trailhead at Elkmont, one of the park's historic sites and campgrounds, to watch this fascinating mating display.

What's up with these bugs? The little beetles live as adults for only twenty-one days, so they have a very short window in which to procreate. Their flashing light, called bioluminescence, is a signal between male and female that encourages females to choose their mates. Why they flash in synchronization is a mystery, but visitors can see this remarkable natural phenomenon in the dead of night as the bugs blink all at once or in waves across hillsides.

The Wildflower National Park

An eye-popping 1,660 flowering plant species all come into bloom in the space of a few months, from spring

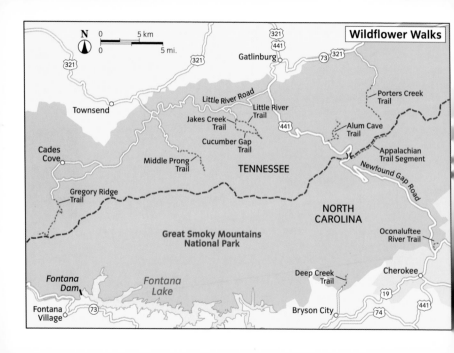

ephemerals that blanket the forest floor with blossoms in April and early May to the rhododendrons that bloom on mountain peaks through early July. With wave after wave of brilliant color, the Great Smoky Mountains burst into spring with a verve that attracts hundreds of thousands of people to its woodland trails, mountain balds, and open meadows.

The best time to enjoy the wildflower spectacle in the park is from mid-March to early May, before leaves appear on the trees and block the sun from the forest floor. Trillium, columbine, lady slipper orchid, bleeding heart, jack-in-the-pulpit, little brown jug, and crested dwarf iris are just a few of the plants in bloom during these months, breaking through last year's leaves in lush waves of color.

Bleeding heart bears some of the spring's most brilliant blooms.

Why Are the Smokies Smoky?

Of the many changes that industrialization brought to the Appalachian region, air quality ranks as one of the most dramatic. The bluish fog over the Great Smoky Mountains, once created by the abundant moisture in the air, now consists primarily of hazy grayish pollution generated by power plants, factories, and automobiles that burn fossil fuels.

Wind currents carry these pollutants into the mountains from the surrounding cities, compromising the scenic views by as much as 80 percent in summer and 40 percent in winter. While visitors can still see 25 miles or more, the near-100-mile views that were possible as recently as fifty years ago have been obscured by tiny airborne sulfate particles. Coal, oil, and gas are the major contributors to the new "smoke" over the Smokies.

Pollutants create a haze over Great Smoky's ridgelines.

Trillium blooms in abundance here every April and May.

To witness the best of the spring wildflowers, try a walk on the Oconaluftee River Trail, a 3-mile stroll with little gain in elevation; or the Deep Creek Trail, also a fairly easy walk that brings you the added bonus of the Indian Creek and Tom Branch waterfalls. Easily accessible by taking Forge Creek Road off the Cades Cove loop road, the Gregory Ridge Trail's first 2 miles offer wonderful views of spring flowers.

Horizons:
Natural and historic sites

Clingmans Dome: The One and Only "Old Smoky"

The best known of the park's mountains, Clingmans Dome is the highest point on the Appalachian Trail and the third-highest peak in the eastern United States. This is the fabled "top of Old Smoky" immortalized in song, and you can drive to within half a mile of the top, where a steep trail takes you up to the 6,643-foot-high summit and an observation tower (another 54 feet above the peak). The view here is worth the climb, extending for 20 miles or more even on hazy days, and for as much as 100 miles when the air is clear. Be sure to bring an extra sweater or jacket and your rainwear, even if the day begins with bright sunshine at lower altitudes, as the temperature

◀ *There's no more photographed view in the park than the vista from Clingmans Dome.*

can drop as much as 20 degrees or more between your starting point and the summit.

Cades Cove: The Driving Loop with Everything

Whether your interest is Appalachian cultural history, peaceful valley scenery, or wildlife in its natural habitat—or all of these—Cades Cove provides exactly the kind of experience you're hoping to find. Here are the former homesteads and town buildings of a mountain community that came together in the early 1800s and remained until the park's formation in 1934, restored with striking accuracy to give visitors as authentic an impression as possible of the people who once farmed this land. You'll see barns, log houses, churches, and a working gristmill where settlers brought their grain

Ski to the Top of the Smokies

Snow or no snow, Clingmans Dome Road is closed every year from December 1 to March 31. You can still hike to the top if you're prepared for changeable weather, or even cross-country-ski there. The crisp, clear winter air may afford a better view than in other seasons.

for milling into the cornmeal they used for baking. Beyond its historical interest, Cades Cove's fertile, grassy valley invites all of the park's wildlife to gather here, making this one of the best places in the Smokies to see black bears, white-tailed deer, groundhogs, skunks, wild turkeys, mink, weasels, and even coyotes. The best time to see the most wildlife is

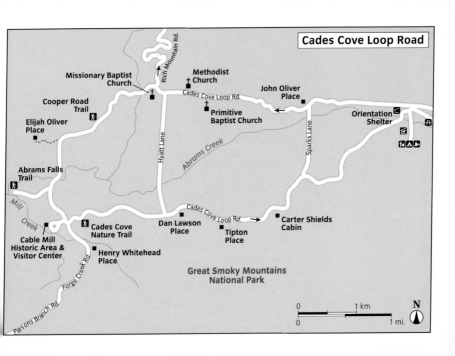

Tipton Place still stands since the days when farmers inhabited Cades Cove.

Crowds do indeed gather on this one-way road, and traffic can be bumper to bumper for hours during June, July, August, and October. The park estimates that 800,000 vehicles drive this road each year, with the vast majority arriving at midday—so if you're stuck in traffic and you'd like a quick escape, take the unpaved Rich Mountain Road to head out of the park to the north, or Parsons Branch Road to exit to the south. Check at the information kiosk before you enter Cades Cove to be sure that these roads are open, as flash flooding can close them temporarily.

early in the morning or late in the day as sunset approaches, when animals are most likely to feed in the open. Oddly enough, these times are not when the largest crowds gather on the 11-mile Cades Cove loop road, so you may have wonderful opportunities to view wildlife at your leisure if you arrive very early.

Cataloochee: The Other Wildlife Valley

As recently as a century ago, one of the largest communities in the Smoky Mountains thrived here in this valley on

ades Cove is one of the park's few open meadowlands.

the east side of the park. Far enough off the park's beaten path to attract fewer tourists than the more accessible Cades Cove and Clingmans Dome, Cataloochee nevertheless offers an equally interesting collection of historic structures and a fine assortment of wildlife, including the best opportunity in the Smokies to see the park's recently introduced elk population.

Peaks surpassing 6,000 feet surround this quiet valley, where two towns—Big Cataloochee and Little Cataloochee—were established just after the Civil War. The townspeople built farms and planted orchards, and the Cataloochee towns prospered and grew to a population of more than 1,200 before the area's conversion to national park status. Today, you can see nine historic buildings in all, including several

This little Methodist church still serves a small congregation today.

homes, a schoolhouse, and a Methodist chapel, both along the road through the valley and down the mile-long Little Cata oochee Trail. Pick up the self-guiding auto tour booklet in a roadside box near the valley entrance for a dollar to enjoy a detailed narrative while you tour the buildings.

It's tricky to get to Cataloochee, but the trip to this tranquil valley can surpass your Cades Cove experience in its ability to deliver wilderness, history, and wildlife. Sixty-five miles from Gatlinburg and 85 miles from Cherokee, Cataloochee requires a long drive down winding, unpaved roads that are safe for cars but not recommended for RVs. The longest route looks the shortest on the map—the road from Gatlinburg into the park on Tennessee Highway 32 becomes a well-maintained gravel road just as it enters the park and crosses the Appalachian Trail into North Carolina, where it continues for more than 30 miles. This winding,

meandering road follows the ridgeline along the northeastern side of the park with dizzying relentlessness, and its one-car width requires even the most daring driver to slow to 10 mph or less on some of the hairpin turns. If you're prone to motion sickness, don't attempt this road (which, by the way, can take as much as two and a half hours to complete). The most direct route into the valley is Interstate 40 to North Carolina exit 20, from

Pipevine swallowtails arrive in flocks in the Cataloochee Valley.

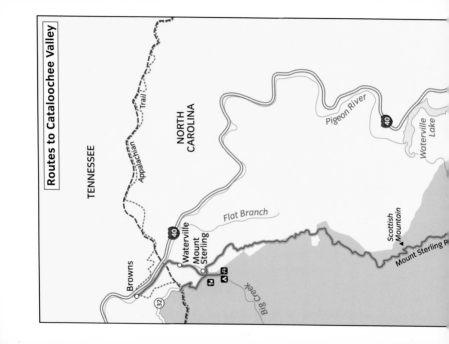

Routes to Cataloochee Valley

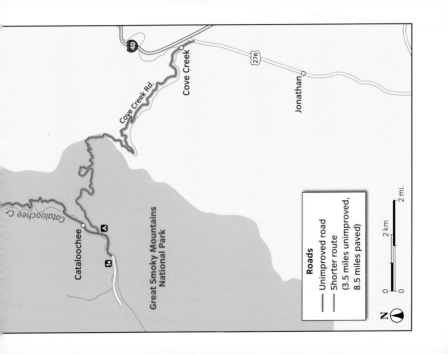

which you'll drive 0.2 mile on North Carolina Highway 276. Turn right onto Cove Creek Road, about 3.5 miles of which are gravel, and follow the signs for 11 miles into the Cataloochee Valley.

Roaring Fork: The Auto Tour with a Difference

There's one more option if you'd like the chance to see both history and wildlife: the Roaring Fork Motor Nature Trail, a paved road that begins near Sugarlands Visitor Center at the park's Gatlinburg entrance. You'll find log cabins here of the sort that were plentiful in these mountains a hundred years ago or more.

The narrow, one-way roadway only opens in summer, but it's closed to buses, trailers, and RVs, so you'll have fewer traffic issues as you wind through the forest. Wildlife viewing takes a different kind of energy here because you're in deep woods instead of a wide clearing. Stop at the Trillium Gap Trailhead to make the 1.25-mile hike to Grotto Falls, one of dozens of small cascades (this one is 25 feet high) throughout the park that create grand displays. If you're ambitious, this trail continues another 4.25 miles to the top of Mount LeConte (6,593 feet).

Oconaluftee and the Mountain Farm Museum

The park's largest concentration of historic buildings is outside the Oconaluftee Visitor Center at the Mountain Farm Museum, where park historians have gathered an assortment of nineteenth-century structures from all over the Smokies. Here you can explore

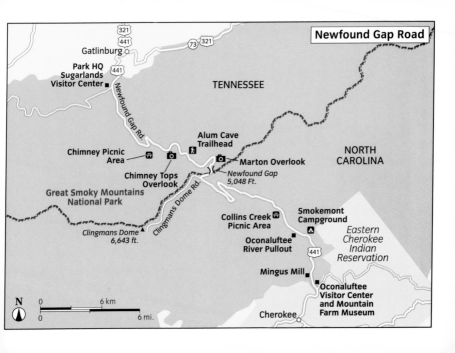

a working blacksmith's shop, an apple storage house, a smokehouse, a log farmhouse, and many other buildings. Costumed interpreters demonstrate period farming methods and household chores.

Costumed interpreters demonstrate farming tasks at the Mountain Farm Museum.

Beat the Crowds on a Quiet Walkway

As you drive along the park's main roads, you'll see signs that suggest an alternative to the jam-packed overlooks and the bumper-to-bumper traffic. Quiet walkways, most of them rarely used, allow you to amble through a forest glade or walk along a bubbling stream in relative calm—and while most of these walkways are close enough to the road that you'll still hear cars during peak seasons, you can enjoy a bit of solitude that most visitors miss. The paths vary in length, but most are shorter than a mile.

Continue half a mile north of the Oconaluftee Visitor Center on Newfound Gap Road to Mingus Mill, a working gristmill that's open daily from mid-March to mid-November. What's special about this mill is that it doesn't use a water wheel—its power comes from a cast-iron turbine system under the building, run by Mingus Creek's rushing water. Not only can you watch a miller grind corn into meal, but you can also purchase that cornmeal to take home.

Look under Mingus Mill to see the ingenious turbine system.

Get Going:
Activities in the park

If you can't find a great way to spend the day in Great Smoky Mountains National Park, you're not trying! Hundreds of miles of hiking trails lead away from the crowds and into the wilderness—and if you're not up for hiking, there's biking, fishing, inner tubing, and just admiring the spectacular scenery.

Hiking

It's the primary activity in the Smokies, and whether you plan to summit the third-highest mountain in the eastern United States, get a workout on a hilly trail, or take a pleasant stroll along a mountain stream, you'll find hikes of every challenge level in this expansive park.

◀ *The Sinks is one of the park's prettiest waterfalls.*

The park's most popular trails include the venerable Appalachian Trail, 70 miles of which cross the park from Deals Gap to the southwest all the way to Big Creek in the northeastern corner. The trail follows the Smokies' famous ridgeline (and the Tennessee–North Carolina border) over Gregory Bald, Thunderhead Mountain, and Clingmans Dome—the highest point on the entire 2,175-mile trail—and then continues through Newfound Gap, and over Charlies Bunion and Mount Guyot.

You'll find some comparatively easy hikes on the Little River Trail, which takes you to the river's headwaters on a wide, fairly level path that begins near Elkmont campground, on the road from Sugarlands Visitor Center to Cades Cove. In spring, you'll have a fine view of the wildflowers on the first 2 miles of this trail as early as mid-March. Extend your walk with the Cucumber Gap and Jakes Creek trails to create a 5-mile loop.

If you have your dog with you, two trails in the park allow leashed pets: Oconaluftee River Trail, a 1.5-mile trail that connects the town of Cherokee, North Carolina, with the Oconaluftee Visitor Center inside the park. The river views make this a popular, well-loved pathway. A very similar path, the Gatlinburg Trail, traces the west prong of the Little Pigeon River from Gatlinburg, Tennessee, to the Sugarlands Visitor Center, offering nearly 2 miles of reasonably level walking.

For real challenge with real payoff, choose any of the five trails that lead to the top of Mount LeConte, the park's third-highest mountain: Alum Cave Trail is the steepest, reaching the summit in 5.5 miles, while Bullhead (7.2 miles) and Boulevard (8 miles) gain elevation more grad

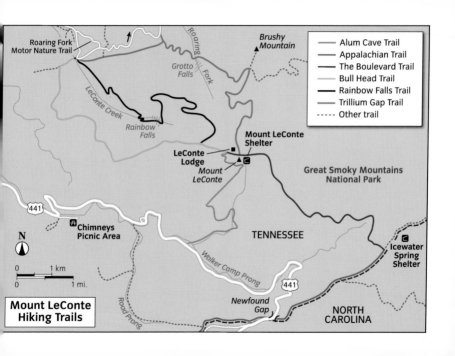

Mount LeConte
Hiking Trails

Roaring Fork
Motor Nature Trail

Brushy Mountain

Grotto Falls

Roaring Fork

LeConte Creek

Rainbow Falls

Mount LeConte Shelter

LeConte Lodge

Mount LeConte

Great Smoky Mountains
National Park

441

Chimneys
Picnic Area

TENNESSEE

Icewater
Spring Shelter

N

Walker Camp Prong

Road Prong

441

Newfound Gap

NORTH
CAROLINA

0   1 km
0   1 mi.

Alum Cave Trail
Appalachian Trail
The Boulevard Trail
Bull Head Trail
Rainbow Falls Trail
Trillium Gap Trail
Other trail

ually. Rainbow Falls and Trillium Gap are 6.5 miles each, and on Monday, Wednesday, and Friday you may encounter llamas and their keepers on Trillium Gap Trail as they bring fresh supplies to the legendary LeConte Lodge at the peak's top.

Bicycling

Cycling is not permitted on park trails, except on the Oconaluftee River and Gatlinburg trails and in Cades Cove. The 11-mile Cades Cove loop road is a favorite cycling route with near-certain opportunities to spot wildlife and enjoy wildflowers, especially in spring. In spring, summer, and fall, the park closes Cades Cove loop road to vehicular traffic on Wednesday and Saturday mornings until 10:00 a.m., giving cyclists a peaceful, auto-free time slot to experience the park's most popular road.

Elevation climbs quickly on many of the park's trails.

Horseback Riding

Bring your own steed or rent one from the park (for about $20 an hour) at one of the four commercial stables in the park near Townsend, Cherokee, and Gatlinburg. More than 500 miles of Great Smoky trails are open to horses, and the park provides camps where you and your horse can stay overnight and be positioned to start down a trail first thing in the morning.

Fishing

With more than 2,100 miles of streams in the park, fishing is a favorite sport here, as most of the waterways are at their full carrying capacity of fish at any time of the year. The Great Smoky Mountains protect one of the last remaining habitats for wild brook trout in the eastern

Horse enthusiasts will find several places to camp with their steeds in and around the park.

United States, and you can fish in any stream or river in the park year-round except for three: Bear Creek at its junction with Forney Creek, Sams Creek where it intersects with Thunderhead Prong, and Indian Flats Prong at the Middle Prong Trail crossing. You'll find

Horse Camps and Where to Rent a Horse

Rent a horse at any of these park-approved stables. Call ahead to reserve your horse.

- **Cades Cove,** near Townsend, Tennessee; (865) 448-6286
- **Smokemont,** near Cherokee, North Carolina; (828) 497-2373
- **Smoky Mountain,** near Gatlinburg, Tennessee; (865) 436-5634
- **Sugarlands,** near Gatlinburg, Tennessee; (865) 436-3535

Camp with your horse at these drive-in horse camps from April through mid-November:

- **Anthony Creek,** 30 miles southeast of Maryville, Tennessee, on U.S. Highway 321
- **Big Creek,** 16 miles east of Newport, Tennessee, on Interstate 40
- **Cataloochee,** off I-40 exit 20; turn right onto Cove Creek Road and follow 11 miles to horse camp
- **Round Bottom,** just north of Cherokee, North Carolina, off U.S. Highway 441
- **Tow String,** 4 miles north of Cherokee, North Carolina, off US 441

(For complete directions see the Web site listed in the Resources chapter.)

all kinds of fishing in the park, including large streams high in the mountains where trout are plentiful, and smallmouth bass concentrations in the lower elevations. Major efforts are in progress in the park to remove the invasive rainbow trout and return the native brook trout to their former numbers—so check with the park to find out what you can catch and keep and what you need to release. You need a valid fishing license from the state in which you plan to fish (see the Resources chapter for where to buy these online). Fishing is allowed from a half hour before official sunrise to a half hour after official sunset.

Fly anglers often choose secluded spots on the Little and Pigeon Rivers.

Swimming and Inner Tubing

These activities can be dangerous on the park's many rivers, creeks, and streams, and park management strongly discourages them. If you want to swim, check out the Townsend "Y," just outside the park in Townsend, where two rivers come together and create a terrific swimming hole. Deep Creek is also a popular place for tubing. White-water rafting is popular outside the park in the Nantahala Gorge, near Cherokee, North Carolina.

The natural swimming hole at the Townsend "Y" is the best place for a cooling dip.

Just for Families

Whether your family loves the active outdoor life or opportunities to learn more about the park in a relaxed setting—or both—you'll find ranger-led walks and talks, hikes at every challenge level, and plenty of opportunities for the whole family to have fun together.

Become a Junior Ranger

Children ages five to twelve can earn a Junior Ranger badge by picking up an age-appropriate booklet ($3) at any of the park's visitor centers and completing the activities inside—or by attending and participating in three ranger-led activities throughout the park. Making a clay pot, bending metal to make a dinner bell at the blacksmith shop, learning to recognize animal tracks, and discovering small mammals in the park are just some of the fun and educational program options available to kids who want to earn the badge.

Ranger-Led Programs

Would you like to learn about the smallest creatures in the park, or splash through a stream to find the tiny animals that live in a hollow log? Choose one of the many nature walks, craft demonstrations, and adventurous hikes offered daily in summer, from the third week in June through the second week in August. Many activities are hands-on, with opportunities to make traditional crafts, meet little woodland creatures face to face, or wade in streams to see what lives below the water's surface. At night, rangers tell stories about the park and the people who once lived there while visitors gather around the campfire, or you can follow a ranger up to the top of Clingmans Dome to watch the sun set. Check the Web site listed in the Resources chapter for events on the day of your visit, or stop at any visitor center's information desk for a list of the day's programs.

Children ages five to twelve can become Junior Rangers by completing some fun activities.

Hey Ranger! Q&A Just for Kids

Q. Do the bears hibernate?

A. Bears in the Smokies don't actually hibernate—that is, they don't go to sleep in the fall and wake up in the spring. The bears do sleep for long periods of time, but a warm spell or a sudden interruption may encourage them to get up and move around, and to forage for food even in the middle of winter. If you're hiking through the park in the colder months, you're not likely to run into a bear, but if it's a warm, sunny day, you just might.

Q. What happened to all the people who lived in these old buildings?

A. Usually people aren't allowed to live in a national park, so when this park was established, the people had to move away. A few of the residents were elderly, and some weren't very well, so they had special permission to stay for the rest of their lives. As for everyone else, some people left the area to find new farmland or jobs in big cities.

Q. Why do the elk have collars?

A. These elk just moved here in 2001, and the park rangers need to keep track of them to be sure they're safe and healthy, so the elk wear special collars with radio transmitters in them. Elk lived here back in the early 1800s (and for many centuries before that), but when the logging industry arrived, most of the trees were cut down, and the elk had nowhere to live. Now there's plenty of good forest and food for elk, so the park has brought them back.

Hayride in Cades Cove

If the thought of sitting in bumper-to-bumper traffic to glimpse a herd of white-tailed deer sounds too much like work, consider an old-fashioned hayride around the 11-mile loop road. Rangers ride along and provide entertaining insights about the cove's history and the people who lived there, and they're quick to spot wildlife you might otherwise miss. Tickets ($8 per person) are available at Cades Cove Stables, near Townsend, Tennessee. Call the stables at (865) 448-6286 for reservations and the hayride schedule.

Hiking

Even the smallest children will love a walk on the Sugarlands Nature Trail, a hike along Alum Creek to find river otters, or a short uphill climb to Juney Whank Falls or Laurel Falls. Many of the park's trails are easy enough for small children (and their pooped parents), and they offer many opportunities to see wildlife up close, from young deer following their mothers to creepy crawlers such as millipedes and salamanders.

Recharge:
Places to sleep and eat

Camping and picnicking are not only encouraged in the Great Smoky Mountains, they're two of the most popular activities in the park. Camping areas are available for car camping, RVs, and hikers with their own bedroll, and eleven official picnic areas provide tables and grills.

Lodging

There's only one lodge in the park, and it's one of the most remote and difficult to access in the entire national park system—which makes it one of the most in demand. LeConte Lodge, high atop Mount LeConte at 6,593 feet, can only be reached by walking up one of five hiking trails, the shortest of which is a steep 5.5 miles. There's no electricity or running water, and the natural quiet is broken only by insects chirping and owls calling at night and birds singing during the days. This summit retreat books up nearly a year in advance—the 12,000 open slots offered each season (mid-March through mid-November) are assigned by lottery in October, and vacancies disappear in a matter of weeks. If you'd like to make a reservation for next year's season, send an e-mail to reservations@lecontelodge.com. Rates run about $100 per night for a cabin, which includes dinner (served promptly at 6:00 p.m.) and a full, hearty breakfast. Two-bedroom lodges, at about $500 per night, sleep eight people or more; and the three-bedroom lodge is about $750 for twelve people, with additional charges for meals. Learn more at www.leconte-lodge.com, or call the lodge office in Sevierville at (865) 429-5704.

Camping

Whether you've arrived in your new RV, you're camping out of your car's trunk, or you yearn for the solitude of the distant mountaintop, the park has the campsite you crave. Ten frontcountry (car-accessible) campgrounds offer hundreds of campsites, all of which have access to cold-water restrooms with flush toilets (there are no showers in the park), and each campsite includes a grill and picnic table. Bring your car or RV, but keep in mind that the campgrounds don't provide electrical or water hook-ups. Of the ten campgrounds, only Cades Cove and Smokemont are open year-round; the others all open in March or April except for Balsam Mountain and Look Rock, which open on the second weekend in May. Most campgrounds close for the season around Halloween except for Elkmont, which remains open until the end of November. Frontcountry camping reservations are taken six months in advance at (877) 444-6777 between 10:00 a.m. and 10:00 p.m. Eastern time daily.

Tent campers will find more than a thousand campsites throughout the park.

Backcountry Campsites

There's no better way to beat the summer crowds than to venture into the backcountry, where the throngs die away and the wilderness opens before you. Campsites in the backcountry are established annually by park staff, and they may change locations each year to minimize the impact on the land, so check at the visitor centers for the current year's sites before you go. There's no charge for use of a backcountry campground, although reservations are suggested as each site sleeps only eight to twenty people. Hiking into a backcountry campsite can provide the kind of wilderness adventure you came to a national park to find, so long as you observe the regulations (see the Resources chapter) and obtain a free backcountry permit. Call the Backcountry Information Office at (865) 436-1297.

Picnicking

Scattered throughout the park are eleven official picnic areas, with individual picnic sites equipped with a table and a raised

Picnic grounds provide a sense of privacy and wonderful scenery.

grill for cooking (bring your own charcoal). These picnic areas are nicely situated in pleasantly scenic spots—alongside a creek or river, or near trailheads that lead to waterfalls, wildflowers, or overlooks—with each site off in its own private nook.

Food Services

There are no restaurants in the park, and the only snack bar/grill is in the camp store at Cades Cove campground, which serves burgers, sausages, sandwiches, ice cream, and soft drinks. Water and soda are available from machines at the Sugarlands and Oconaluftee Visitor Centers. Bring your own picnic supplies and camp food—and store anything you don't eat in the trunk of your car to keep it out of sight of inquisitive bears.

Beyond the Borders:
Off-Site Places to sleep, eat, and go

If you've ever felt, even for a moment, that you do not fully appreciate the wonder of untouched wilderness and the richness that natural spaces offer to our society, make the drive through Sevierville, Pigeon Forge, and Gatlinburg, Tennessee, the supercharged resort towns on U.S. Highway 441, as you approach Great Smoky Mountains National Park. Then pass traffic light number 10 in Gatlinburg and drive on the tree-lined road into the pristine national park beyond . . . and the sense of overwhelming relief you feel will tell you all you need to know about the value of America's parklands.

You may cringe at the contrast, but without these centers of entertainment, nightlife, lodging, and restaurants, Great Smoky might not be the most visited park in the nation—in fact, its visitation figures might drop alarmingly without these havens for vacationers who do not choose to camp. Gatlinburg alone, with its hotels, cabins, and inns that can accommodate a total of 35,000 guests on a single night, brings millions of people to nature's doorstep every summer and fall. So before we look askance at Gatlinburg and its hyper-commercial neighbor, Pigeon Forge, we must appreciate the full vacation experience they make possible.

Leave Interstate 40 at exit 407 and drive into Sevierville (that's se-VEER-ville), passing half a dozen "welcome centers" (see the "Beware the Time-Share Hustlers" sidebar in this chapter) as you motor through town and noting the increasing number of billboards, banners, and advertising placards. Suddenly you're past Sevierville, and you begin to sense a change in the atmosphere. Bright, moving neon displays come into view. Flashing, animated video signs implore you

to stop and buy tickets to any number of dinner shows and attractions—comedy revues, religious revivals, down-home Southern entertainment, even an all-singing breakfast show—while glittering, neon-rimmed amusements whiz by one after the other. Go-karts, a dozen variations on minigolf, thrill rides, whirling gizmos, and innumerable tourist-trap souvenir shops virtually shout to you as you pass. This is Pigeon Forge, a town that packs a whole lot of man-made diversions into just a couple of miles.

Then a little miracle happens—you're out of town, and the crazy lights, car horns, and loud music are gone. You've entered a 4-mile stretch called the "spur," a connecting road through undeveloped land much like the park you've come to see. Tall, densely foliated trees surround you, and cicadas chirp in an eerie rhythm. You roll your window down to

he neon-powered lunacy that is Pigeon Forge stretches for 3 miles.

smell the clear scent of hardwoods and chlorophyll, and to listen for the "Who cooks for you?" call of a barred owl.

The trees fall away as you enter Gatlinburg—and after Pigeon Forge, this town is downright quaint, a village with narrower streets and packed-together shops. You'll see all the T-shirt stores and hillbilly-themed gift shops you can stand—not to mention an amazing number of wedding chapels, plus places to rent a wedding gown as well as a tuxedo—but in between these are small stores that feature locally made crafts, specialty items like hemp products, and gifts made from other natural materials; bizarre attractions like the Ripley's Believe It or Not! Museum, the Guinness World of Records, and Cooters in the Smokies, a service station where you can see the General Lee, the car from the TV show *The Dukes of Hazzard;* and another

half-dozen variations on minigolf (including the imaginative Hillbilly Golf, which sends you up a 300-foot incline railway to hit your ball past "mountaineer obstacles" like old-fashioned outhouses and stills). Rib joints and trout restaurants, bluegrass and mountain music played on the streets (you can listen for free), and all the fun you can handle make Gatlinburg a darned appealing place to spend an evening or a week's worth of evenings, in stunning but surprisingly agreeable contrast to the wilderness not 10 feet from its last traffic light.

Where to Stay in Gatlinburg

There are far more hotel rooms than there are residents in this town, so it's easy to miss a unique, romantic, or authentically Southern Mountain lodging

Beware the Time-Share Hustlers!

Everywhere in Gatlinburg, Pigeon Forge, and Sevierville, you'll see signs that promise discount tickets to major attractions. What's really going on? Every one of these fronts is managed by salespeople who are paid to pressure you into attending a presentation on time-shares and travel clubs. The discounts you receive on tickets to Dixie Stampede or Ripley's Aquarium, for example, may be negligible—or nonexistent, as our test case proved (we actually paid more than we would have at the door), and the ninety-minute or longer presentation required is hardly the way you planned to spend your precious vacation time.

Be especially careful in Sevierville! *Stop only at the visitor center with the National Park Service logo on the sign out front*. The others are all time-share sales offices.

Go to this welcome center in Sevierville, and skip the others you'll see there.

option. For additional choices other than the standouts listed here, visit www.gatlinburgtnhotel.com.

Bearskin Lodge on the River (840 River Road; 877-795-7546 or 865-430-4330; www.thebearskinlodge.com). This fairly new hotel furnishes its guest rooms in rustic lodge style, but the amenities are anything but primitive—fireplaces, whirlpool tubs, private balconies for every room, and a view of the Little Pigeon River. Prices range from $50 to $250, depending on season and room choice.

Buckhorn Inn (2140 Tudor Mountain Road; 865-436-4668; www.buckhorninn.com). This 1938 inn reflects Gatlinburg's earliest days as a vacation destination, with its killer views of the mountains and its open, airy common rooms traditionally furnished with big, comfortable chairs and sitting areas. Guests can choose a traditional room ($115–$130)

a premier room ($175), or even a private cottage or guest house ($175–$320).

Eight Gables Inn Bed and Breakfast (219 North Mountain Trail; 800-279-5716 or 865-430-3344; www.eightgables.com). This elegant inn is for people who prefer a more genteel style of Southern hospitality. Contemporary furnishings mix with wood-paneled walls and hardwood floors to create a sense of sophistication throughout the inn that extends to its award-winning grounds. A housekeeper turns down your comforter-topped bed each evening, and amenities include fireplaces, oversized whirlpool tubs, and bathrobes in every room. $140–$190 for standard rooms, $210–$270 for suites.

The Lodge at Buckbury Creek (961 Campbell Lead Road; 865-430-8030 www.buckberrylodge.com). Crossing Adirondack architecture with Smoky Mountain scenery, this lodge is one of the most luxurious in the Gatlinburg area—which means it's not for every budget. If you're looking for a secluded, romantic getaway, however, this is just the place: Even the smallest suites ($180–$265) have fireplaces, comfy couches, and bathrooms with soaking tubs. The grand suites ($300–$460) are larger and more lavishly appointed than most people's homes, and they feature decks with expansive mountain views.

Mountain Heritage Inn (575 River Road; 800-343-7953 or 865-436-3474; www.mountainheritageinn.com). Locally owned and a walkable half block from the bustle of the Parkway, this pleasant hotel features refrigerators in every room, hot tubs, and just enough distance from the central "strip" to promise you a good night's sleep. Rates are $40–$129, based on the season and room choice.

Where to Eat in Gatlinburg

You came to Gatlinburg for down-home country cooking, and you'll find it in just about every restaurant on the strip. While the selection is not broad, it's definitely deep, and you'll soon find yourself up to your neck in barbecued ribs, trout prepared any way you like, and all the pancakes you can eat. The best news: Casual dress is the norm, and none of these restaurants expect you to dress for dinner. Listed here are some of the most delicious eateries.

Applewood Farmhouse Restaurant (1151 Parkway, at traffic light number 10; 865-436-4669). Here you can get the best down-home country breakfast in town. The apple fritters and apple muffins are a house specialty, served with homemade apple butter—and every guest gets an apple julep, a special concoction of four fruit juices (the recipe is available for the asking). Open daily 8:00 a.m.–9:00 p.m. (until 10:00 p.m. on Friday and Saturday). Closed Christmas, and Monday and Thursday in January and February. Lunch $6–$9; dinner $13–$20.

Atrium Pancakes (432 Parkway, next to Best Western Crossroads Inn; 865-430-3684). Light, fluffy pancakes in more than twenty-five varieties are served with Southern charm at this breakfast and lunch eatery. Try the Caribbean pancakes, loaded with fresh bananas and coconut, or the Red, White, and Blue Roll-Ups, stuffed with fresh fruit and topped with real whipped cream. Known best for its Belgian waffles and French toast, the Atrium serves owner/chef Don Smith's own homemade syrup, as well as the pies, salads, and dressings he concocts personally. Open daily 7:00 a.m.–2:00 p.m. Breakfast and lunch $6–$10.

Bennett's Pit Bar-B-Que (714 River Road, on U.S. Highway 441 at traffic light number 5; 865-436-2400). With ribs around every corner in Gatlinburg, how can you tell which are best? You'll find them here at Bennett's, where the smoky-sweet ribs are deep pink and tender enough to fall off the bone. Pulled pork shoulder is the house specialty— order it with the baked beans, which have never seen the inside of a can. Finish your meal with apple cobbler and vanilla bean ice cream. The picniclike atmosphere is fun for the whole family. Open daily 8:00 a.m.–10:00 p.m.; hours may vary in winter. Closed Christmas. Lunch $6–$11; dinner $8–$20.

Calhoun's (1004 Parkway, near the park entrance; 865-436-4100). Go for the award-winning ribs, but be sure to order one or both of the two signature side dishes: Spinach Maria, a spicy side that

Calhoun's makes one of the best strawberry shortcakes you'll find anywhere.

unites the leafy veggie with at least four kinds of cheese; and Tennessee Corn Puddin', a modern take on the old-time creamed dish. Then let your server talk you into the best strawberry shortcake you've ever had, layered with two big slabs of real butter shortbread, chantilly cream, and fresh berries. Open 11:00 a.m.–10:30 p.m. Monday–Thursday, 11:00 a.m.–11:00 p.m. Friday, 11:00 a.m.–11:30 p.m. Saturday, and 11:00 a.m.–10:00 p.m. Sunday. Lunch and dinner $8–$20.

Howard's Restaurant (976 Parkway, between traffic lights 9 and 10; 865-436-3600). The closest thing you'll find to upscale continental fare on the Parkway, Howard's serves a fine selection of entrees, from its own versions of Smoky Mountain rainbow trout to a Steak for Two plate with an astonishing twenty-eight ounces of beef. Salads that dare to venture beyond iceberg lettuce, homemade blue cheese dressing, and a grown-up atmosphere make this a nice oasis in a boisterous town. Serving lunch and dinner daily 11:00 a.m.–10:00 p.m. (Friday and Saturday until 11:00 p.m.). Lunch $7–$12; dinner $12–$30.

Pancake Pantry (628 Parkway, between traffic lights 6 and 7; 865-436-4724). There's almost always a line down the block to get into this favorite breakfast place in the morning—and it's no wonder, with pancakes served more than twenty different ways. Sandwiches and salads as well as pancakes are served at lunch. Open daily 7:00 a.m.–4:00 p.m. Closed Thanksgiving and Christmas. Breakfast and lunch $7–$10.

Smoky Mountain Trout House (410 North Parkway, just north of traffic light number 3; 865-436-5416). The rainbow trout served here is raised on the proprietor's trout farm, and it's dished up in more than a dozen different ways. Try the traditional pan-fried variety for a fresh, crispy taste of the Smokies. Open for dinner only from 5:00 to 10:00 p.m. (9:00 p.m. in winter) daily. $12–$17.

What to Do

Gatlinburg is stuffed with so many attractions that we can't possibly list them all, so here are some you should not miss, as well as some top experiences in Great Smoky's other gateways.

Great Smoky Arts and Crafts Community (Gatlinburg, Tennessee; 800-565-7330; www.artsandcraftscommunity .com). When you've bought all of the souvenir baseball caps and shot glasses you can carry, take the Gatlinburg Trolley's Yellow line ($1 for an all-day pass) up U.S. Highway 321 and into a completely different atmosphere. Area artists welcome you to their studios and galleries, where they display pottery, paintings, fiber arts, basketry, wood carving, metal arts, jewelry, candles, and much more. Watch the artists at work and see them create the traditional and modern crafts, many of them inspired by the region's beauty and raw materials. You're sure to take away a unique item or two—or six.

Ripley's Aquarium of the Smokies (88 River Road, at traffic light number 5 on the Parkway, Gatlinburg, Tennessee; 865-430-8808). You may balk at the $19.99 price tag per adult ($10.99 for children six to eleven and $4.99 for children two to five), but once you've ridden the moving walkway through the 340-foot-long shark lagoon, you'll be delighted that you came. This astonishing acrylic tank arches over you just inches from your head and flanks you on either side, bringing 12-foot sharks, tarpons, stingrays, barracudas, and those huge, creepy sawfish right up to your nose. Touch tanks with horseshoe crabs and stingrays, a gallery of the sea's most colorful and beautiful creatures (like jellyfish, octopi, and corals), and half-size

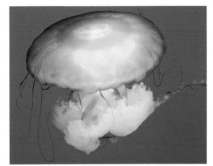

A deep-sea aquarium in Tennessee? Ripley's Aquarium provides jaw-dropping looks at sea creatures with some educational value tucked in.

displays that allow children to surround themselves with tropical wonders all make this aquarium a big hit with young kids—with just enough educational material to please their parents.

Tuckaleechee Caverns (825 Cavern Road, just off US 321, Townsend,

Tennessee; 865-448-2274). While there are caves in the national park, most are off-limits to visitors, so these caverns provide the best opportunity to see the Great Smoky Mountains from the inside. Cave onyx, flowstone, stalagmites (pointing up) and stalactites (pointing down), cave draperies, and helictites are just a few of the amazing formations you'll see inside this 300-million-year-old hole in the earth. Open daily March 15–November 15. March and November: 10:00 a.m.–5:00 p.m.; April through October: 9:00 a.m.–6:00 p.m. Adults $12, children five to eleven $6, children four and younger free.

Museum of the Cherokee Indian (U.S. Highway 441 and Drama Road, Cherokee, North Carolina; 828-497-3481). At the other end of Newfound Gap Road lies a thousand years of history, blending ancient Indian mythology with the all too real facts of the Cherokees' nineteenth-century dismissal from their homeland. This well-executed museum on the Qualla Reservation—the home of the Eastern Band of Cherokee Indians—uses holographic images, storytelling, traditional displays, and hundreds of artifacts to give modern visitors a sense of the Cherokee way of life in the distant past, in recent history, and today. Once you've seen the museum, continue on to the Oconaluftee Indian Village, where history comes to life as reenactors in traditional dress demonstrate pottery making, building a dugout canoe, beadwork, basketmaking, finger weaving, and more. End your day here with *Unto These Hills*, the outdoor drama that retells Cherokee history under the stars. The museum is open daily 9:00 a.m.–7:00 p.m.; closed Christmas, Thanksgiving, and New Year's Day. Adults $9, children six to thirteen $6, children five and younger free.

Resources

Backcountry camping information and regulations: (865) 436-1297 (Backcountry Information Office); www.nps.gov/grsm/planyourvisit/backcountry-regs.htm.

Bird checklist (includes 240 species): www.nps.gov/grsm/naturescience/birds-checklist.htm.

Horse camp reservations, regulations, directions, and more: www.nps.gov/grsm/planyourvisit/horsecamps.htm.

LeConte Lodge: (865) 429-5704 (lodge office in Sevierville); reservations@lecontelodge.com; www.leconte-lodge.com.

Schedule of events: www.nps.gov/grsm/planyourvisit/events.htm.

Weather Webcam: www.nps.gov/grsm/photosmultimedia. Here you can check the park's weather and view images from the park's western and eastern ends. Click on the Webcam links for Look Rock and Purchase Knob to see temperature, wind speed, and air quality readings. The images are updated every fifteen minutes.

Other Helpful Resources

Cherokee Chamber of Commerce: (877) 433-6700; www.cherokeesmokies.com.

Fishing licenses (Tennessee): www.wildlifelicense.com/tn/.

Fishing licenses (North Carolina): www.ncwildlife.org/pg01_License/pg1a.asp.

Gatlinburg Chamber of Commerce: (800) 568-4748; www.gatlinburgtnhotel.com or www.gatlinburg.com.

Gatlinburg Lodging and Hospitality Association: www.gatlinburgtnhotel.com. A good resource for condo and cabin rentals in Gatlinburg, Tennessee.

Great Smoky Mountains Association: (888) 892-9102 or (865) 436-6884; www.smokiesstore.org.

Townsend Chamber of Commerce: (865) 425-0833; www.townsendchamber.org.

Index

91

INDEX

FALCONGUIDES®

Copyright © 2008 Morris Book Publishing, LLC

Falcon and FalconGuides are registered trademarks of Morris Book Publishing, LLC.
PopOut is a trademark of Compass Maps, Ltd.
popout™ map and associated products are the subject of patents pending worldwide.

Photos on pages 23 and 34 courtesy of National Park Service
Text design by Mary Ballachino
Maps created by XNR Productions, Inc. © Morris Book Publishing, LLC

Library of Congress Cataloging–in–Publication Data is available.
ISBN 978-0-7627-4806-8

Printed in China
10 9 8 7 6 5 4 3 2 1

The author and The Globe Pequot Press assume no liability for accidents happening to, or injuries sustained by, readers who engage in the activities described in this book.